Wolfgang Ama[...]

MOZAR[.]

CORONATION MASS

K. 317

(Taubmann)

Vocal Score

Klavierauszug

PETRUCCI LIBRARY PRESS

CONTENTS

ORCHESTRA

2 Oboes, 2 Bassoons
2 Horns, 2 Trumpets, 3 Trombones, Timpani
Organ
Violin I, Violin II, Violoncello, Double Bass

Duration: ca. 30 minutes
First performance: Easter Sunday, April 4, 1779
Salzburg Cathedral
Soli, Chorus and Orchestra with the composer directing

Complete orchestral parts compatible with this vocal score are available (Cat. No. A2694) from
E. F. Kalmus & Co., Inc.
6403 West Rogers Circle
Boca Raton, FL 33487 USA
(800) 434 - 6340
www.kalmus-music.com

Mass in C major "Coronation"

K. 317

Wolfgang Amadeus Mozart (1756–1791)
Piano reduction by Otto Taubmann

Credo

Sanctus

Benedictus

Agnus Dei

9 781608 741205